Llangunnor Hill: a loco-descriptive poem. With notes.

John Bethell

Llangunnor Hill: a loco-descriptive poem. With notes.
Bethell, John
ESTCID: T123964
Reproduction from British Library
Anonymous. By John Bethell. With an additional titlepage.
Carmarthen : printed and sold for the author by J. Daniel. Sold also by Messrs. B. and J. White, London; Mr. Browne, Bristol; Mr. J. J. Hugh, Glocester; Mr. Potter, Haverfordwest; Mr. Wilmot, Pembroke; and Mr. Owen, Swansea, [1794].
xii,28p. ; 8°

Eighteenth Century
Collections Online
Print Editions

Gale ECCO Print Editions

Relive history with *Eighteenth Century Collections Online*, now available in print for the independent historian and collector. This series includes the most significant English-language and foreign-language works printed in Great Britain during the eighteenth century, and is organized in seven different subject areas including literature and language; medicine, science, and technology; and religion and philosophy. The collection also includes thousands of important works from the Americas.

The eighteenth century has been called "The Age of Enlightenment." It was a period of rapid advance in print culture and publishing, in world exploration, and in the rapid growth of science and technology – all of which had a profound impact on the political and cultural landscape. At the end of the century the American Revolution, French Revolution and Industrial Revolution, perhaps three of the most significant events in modern history, set in motion developments that eventually dominated world political, economic, and social life.

In a groundbreaking effort, Gale initiated a revolution of its own: digitization of epic proportions to preserve these invaluable works in the largest online archive of its kind. Contributions from major world libraries constitute over 175,000 original printed works. Scanned images of the actual pages, rather than transcriptions, recreate the works ***as they first appeared.***

Now for the first time, these high-quality digital scans of original works are available via print-on-demand, making them readily accessible to libraries, students, independent scholars, and readers of all ages.

For our initial release we have created seven robust collections to form one the world's most comprehensive catalogs of 18th century works.

Initial Gale ECCO Print Editions collections include:

> ***History and Geography***
> Rich in titles on English life and social history, this collection spans the world as it was known to eighteenth-century historians and explorers. Titles include a wealth of travel accounts and diaries, histories of nations from throughout the world, and maps and charts of a world that was still being discovered. Students of the War of American Independence will find fascinating accounts from the British side of conflict.

Social Science
Delve into what it was like to live during the eighteenth century by reading the first-hand accounts of everyday people, including city dwellers and farmers, businessmen and bankers, artisans and merchants, artists and their patrons, politicians and their constituents. Original texts make the American, French, and Industrial revolutions vividly contemporary.

Medicine, Science and Technology
Medical theory and practice of the 1700s developed rapidly, as is evidenced by the extensive collection, which includes descriptions of diseases, their conditions, and treatments. Books on science and technology, agriculture, military technology, natural philosophy, even cookbooks, are all contained here.

Literature and Language
Western literary study flows out of eighteenth-century works by Alexander Pope, Daniel Defoe, Henry Fielding, Frances Burney, Denis Diderot, Johann Gottfried Herder, Johann Wolfgang von Goethe, and others. Experience the birth of the modern novel, or compare the development of language using dictionaries and grammar discourses.

Religion and Philosophy
The Age of Enlightenment profoundly enriched religious and philosophical understanding and continues to influence present-day thinking. Works collected here include masterpieces by David Hume, Immanuel Kant, and Jean-Jacques Rousseau, as well as religious sermons and moral debates on the issues of the day, such as the slave trade. The Age of Reason saw conflict between Protestantism and Catholicism transformed into one between faith and logic -- a debate that continues in the twenty-first century.

Law and Reference
This collection reveals the history of English common law and Empire law in a vastly changing world of British expansion. Dominating the legal field is the *Commentaries of the Law of England* by Sir William Blackstone, which first appeared in 1765. Reference works such as almanacs and catalogues continue to educate us by revealing the day-to-day workings of society.

Fine Arts
The eighteenth-century fascination with Greek and Roman antiquity followed the systematic excavation of the ruins at Pompeii and Herculaneum in southern Italy; and after 1750 a neoclassical style dominated all artistic fields. The titles here trace developments in mostly English-language works on painting, sculpture, architecture, music, theater, and other disciplines. Instructional works on musical instruments, catalogs of art objects, comic operas, and more are also included.

The BiblioLife Network

This project was made possible in part by the BiblioLife Network (BLN), a project aimed at addressing some of the huge challenges facing book preservationists around the world. The BLN includes libraries, library networks, archives, subject matter experts, online communities and library service providers. We believe every book ever published should be available as a high-quality print reproduction; printed on-demand anywhere in the world. This insures the ongoing accessibility of the content and helps generate sustainable revenue for the libraries and organizations that work to preserve these important materials.

The following book is in the "public domain" and represents an authentic reproduction of the text as printed by the original publisher. While we have attempted to accurately maintain the integrity of the original work, there are sometimes problems with the original work or the micro-film from which the books were digitized. This can result in minor errors in reproduction. Possible imperfections include missing and blurred pages, poor pictures, markings and other reproduction issues beyond our control. Because this work is culturally important, we have made it available as part of our commitment to protecting, preserving, and promoting the world's literature.

GUIDE TO FOLD-OUTS MAPS and OVERSIZED IMAGES

The book you are reading was digitized from microfilm captured over the past thirty to forty years. Years after the creation of the original microfilm, the book was converted to digital files and made available in an online database.

In an online database, page images do not need to conform to the size restrictions found in a printed book. When converting these images back into a printed bound book, the page sizes are standardized in ways that maintain the detail of the original. For large images, such as fold-out maps, the original page image is split into two or more pages

Guidelines used to determine how to split the page image follows:

- Some images are split vertically; large images require vertical and horizontal splits.
- For horizontal splits, the content is split left to right.
- For vertical splits, the content is split from top to bottom.
- For both vertical and horizontal splits, the image is processed from top left to bottom right.

LLANGUNNOR HILL:

A LOCO-DESCRIPTIVE POEM.

WITH NOTES.

"Happy the man, who to these shades retires,
"Whom nature charms, and whom the muse inspires,
"Whom humble joys of home felt quiet please,
"Successive study, industry, and ease
"Ye sacred Nine! that all my soul possess,
"Whose raptures fire me, and whose visions bless,
"Bear me, oh bear me, to sequester'd scenes,
"The bow'ry mazes, and surrounding greens,
"To Towy's banks, which fragrant breezes fill,
"And to the Muses on LLANGUNNOR HILL."

           Altered from POPE's WINDSOR FOREST.

CARMARTHEN,

PRINTED AND SOLD FOR THE AUTHOR BY J. DANIEL.

SOLD ALSO

BY MESSRS. B. AND J. WHITE, FLEET-STREET, LONDON, MR. BROWNE, BRISTOL, MR. J. J. HOUGH, GLOCESTER, MR. POTTER, HAVERFORDWEST, MR. WILMOT, PEMBROKE, AND MR. OWEN, SWANSEA.

LLANGUNNOR HILL:

A

LOCO-DESCRIPTIVE POEM.

WITH NOTES.

HUMBLY DEDICATED BY THE AUTHOR

TO THE PUBLIC AT LARGE.

CONTINUI MONTES NI DISSOCIENTUR OPACA
VALLE SED UT VENIENS DEXTRUM LATUS ASPICIAT SOL,
LÆVUM DISCEDENS CURRU FUGIENTE VAPORET
TEMPERIEM LAUDES HOR.

IMITATION

Form in your own expanded mind,
A mighty chain of hills combin'd,
  Between a shady valley fair
The right, receives Sol's rising beams,
The left his evening's ardent gleams,
  Whilst pure and temperate is the air.

CARMARTHEN,
PRINTED AND SOLD FOR THE AUTHOR BY J. DANIEL.

PREFACE.

IF an experienced author, who has published a new performance, even on an ordinary subject, feels himself deeply impressed with awe, when he submits his production to the judgment of the public, what must be the sensations of the unpractised writer of the following sheets, who has presumed to venture on a less beaten track, and to submit the fruits of his industry to the scrutinizing eye of so respectable a body? The feelings of that writer may be better conceived, than described. but conscious of having exerted his best abilities, slender as they are, in the execution of the task thus voluntarily undertaken, (however imperfectly that task may appear to be discharged) he submits, with respectful deference, not only to his judges, but to such sentence as they shall find it necessary to pronounce on the present occasion He has, in truth, some reason to hope, that, on account of his inexperience as an author, and the considerable number of local objects which the work now presented professes to delineate, independent of such other subjects and reflections as are occasionally introduced, a liberal allowance will be made for those imperfections which superior abilities may detect, and from which human productions are rarely, if ever, exempt. CANDOR will, doubtless, be ready to acknowledge that it is infinitely more easy for a limner to excel in painting a single portrait, than in preserving and describing the exact lineaments of various faces thrown together upon canvass, in one connected view. CANDOR will

> " Survey the whole, nor seek slight faults to find
> " Where nature moves, and rapture warms the mind,
> " Whoever thinks a faultless piece to see,
> " Thinks what ne'er was, nor is, nor e'er shall be "
> POPE's Essay on Criticism

In the composition of a descriptive poem, proper regard seems necessary to be had to one essential requisite, technically called CUSTOM, for the purpose of preserving perspicuity, and general good sense Destitute of that advantage, unlimited fancy would often furnish entertainment for the eyes, rather than the mind. It would extend at once into different parts of nature, and of life, and gather an assemblage of ideas, from which it would be difficult to select the most striking. But duly restrained, the

PREFACE.

the poet's efforts, like the mariner's compass, would ultimately fix on some decisive point. The poet, therefore, whose aim is to describe both nature and art, must seek his ornaments from their sources, as intimately interwoven with the scene he endeavors to paint, and graces will thence arise, (if he possesses taste to cull them with judgment) not only suitable to, but amply sufficient for, his primary design

The opinions of many learned men on the subject of descriptive poetry, and its occasional embellishments, having differed considerably when their abilities were exercised in examining the productions of authors of the first literary eminence, presented a difficulty of choice in regard to the plan and execution of the subsequent undertaking It has been the object of the writer to profit by the sentiments of professed critics, given on works similar to his own, and by avoiding either extreme, to pursue, as far as his judgment enabled him, an intermediate course How far he has succeeded in that endeavor, is humbly submitted to the decision of a generous public,

By their devoted servant,

SEPTEMBER 5, 1794

THE AUTHOR.

CONTENTS.

THE introduction, which contains an eulogium on Mr. Dyer, author of the poem on Grongar Hill - - - page 1

Description of the river Towy, its occasional floods, and the farmer's care in securing his property in the valley from inundation - - 2

————————Llangunnor church-yard, which, leading to the subject of equality in the grave, introduces reflections on the dangerous tendency of the prevalent doctrines in France - - - 3

————————The happiness of Britons, in being far removed from the actual seat of war, enjoying the sweets of domestic quiet in their native soil, with a recommendation to unanimity, as the means of opposing the evil effects of the doctrines mentioned above, preserving the life of our amiable sovereign, and upholding our most excellent constitution - 5

Apology for this digression - - - 6

Description of various appearances of nature, and the employment of husbandmen, in the autumnal season, when the scene of the poem is laid. 6 & 7

————————Cystanog woods - - - 7

————————The harmony of the birds there, conveying a lesson of morality - - - ibid

Descrip-

Description of the waters of Towy, reflecting back the noontide sun-beams - - p'ge 7
——————The windings of that river, resembling them to the vicissitudes of human life, with suitable reflections - - - - ibid
——————Cystanog-House - - - 8
——————The Bishop's-Palace, which having been the residence of the late bishop of St David's, and present bishop of Rochester, introduces an eulogium on him for his able opposition to Dr. Priestley, in defence of the Christian faith, and also for his zeal in promoting an increase of the stipends of the curates in the first-mentioned diocese   8 & 9
——————Castle-Piggin - - - - 9
——————Penybank - - - - ibid
——————Abergwilly church - - - 10
————————————village - - - ibid
——————Druslwyn castle - - - - ibid
——————Pen'ralltfawr - - - - ibid
——————Allt-y-Gôg - - - - 11
——————The cottages of the peasants, with reflections on the blameless tenor of their lives. - ibid
——————The corn standing in stacks in the fields, yielding a prospect of plenty - - - ibid
——————The gleaners, concluding with a recommendation to husbandmen to throw them, Boaz-like, a liberal handful - - - - 12
——————The reward of such charity - ibid
——————The sport of angling - - - 13
——————Netting for partridges - - - ibid

Descrip-

CONTENTS.

Description of the river Gwilly emptying itself into Towy, and thereby teaching a lesson of obedience to the higher powers - - page 14

——————Towy obeying that lesson, and ultimately submitting to discharge itself into the main ocean - - - - ibid

——————Dan-yr-Allt - - ibid

——————The river Towy flowing near it - ibid

——————A cascade - - - 15

——————A new Villa near Carmarthen ibid

——————Penlan mansion-house - - 16

——————The beauteous clumps of fir-trees near it - - - - - ibid

——————The iron furnaces and other works near the river Towy - - - ibid

——————The benefits accruing from industry ibid

——————The parade, which introduces a panegyric on the fair sex - - - 16 & 17

——————Llwyn-y-Gwragedd Hill - 17

——————The sport of hare-hunting, with reflections arising from it - - - - 18

——————The mine-works, near Llwyn-y-Gwragedd, and the delusive prospects they sometimes hold out to mine-adventurers - - ibid

——————The advantages of small successes in mining, which contribute to perseverance, and occasionally terminate in good fortune - 19

——————Maeslan - - - - ibid

——————Tyllwyd - - - - ibid

——————White-House, formerly the residence of

CONTENTS.

Sir Richard Steele, which introduces a tribute to his memory - - page 19 & 20

Description of White-House orchard, in an arbor in which, tradition says, Sir Richard Steele wrote his comedy of the " Conscious Lovers" - 20

————————Mount-Pleasant - - 21

————————Carmarthen church-tower, a passing bell tolling in it, which introduces appropriate reflections - - - ibid

————————The town of Carmarthen, the birth place of the prophet Merlin, who lived in a cave in Allt-Fyrddin Hill . - - 22 & 23

————————Carmarthen castle - - 23

————————Ships moored near Carmarthen quay, others coming up to it on the influx, and some preparing for sea, on the reflux of the tide - ibid

————————The benefits of the tide, with relation to commerce, and suitable reflections on the wisdom and power of the Creator, displayed in regulating its motions - - - - ibid

————————Fishermen on the river, pursuing their ordinary calling - - - 25

————————Their coracles, and modes of using and carrying them - - - ibid

————————Job's-Well, and the death of its recent owner in the prime of life, which introduces an eulogium on the character of his father 25 & 26

————————Treberfed - - - 27

————————A modern built cottage near Pontcarreg mill - - - - - - - ibid

Descrip-

CONTENTS.

Description of Rhydgorse - - page 27
————————The combined studies of a gentleman occasionally resident there - 27 & 28
Eulogium on the judges of the superior courts, for the impartial manner in which they administer justice - - - 28
Conclusion - - - ibid

LLANGUNNOR

LLANGUNNOR HILL:

A LOCO-DESCRIPTIVE POEM.

WHEN Dyer, fraught with heav'nly fire,
On Grongar touch'd his charming lyre,
With wonder gaz'd the list'ning swains,
Surpriz'd to hear his tender strains,
And fix'd and wedded to the spot, 5
Their rustic labors quite forgot!
Struck with the sweetness of his lays,
My muse this grateful tribute pays,
Ere she begins, with feeble skill,
To celebrate Llangunnor Hill. 10

Ver 1,2] Grongar is a hill situated in the parish of Llangathen, in Carmarthenshire, that commands a delightful view of the charming vale of Towy, and which hill is the subject of a beautiful poem, written by Mr Dyer, and published in his works

Ver 10] Llangunnor Hill is in Llangunnor parish, in the above county, and within a mile of its principal town, Carmarthen. In justification of the author's prejudice in favor of this hill, and the prospects it commands, those who have not been upon the spot, may refer to the Epistolary Correspondence of Sir Richard Steele, vol. 1. p 244.

Llangunnor! near whose verdant side,
Thy waters, Towy! smoothly glide,
Winding along the vale below,
With pace, majestically flow.
Save when tremendous thunders roll,   15
(Terrific to the guilty soul!)
And streams of vivid lightning fly,
Illuminating earth and sky,
And, in succession, rain, in rills,
Rolls down in torrents from the hills;   20
Then floods unite their mighty force,
With speed to urge thee in thy course,

Ver. 12] The river Towy, takes its rise in Cardiganshire, and running from north to south, in various serpentine directions, extremely grateful to the eye, passes by the towns of Llandovery and Llandilo-fawr, thence by Dinevor Castle, (the royal seat of the princes of South Wales whilst they flourished, and which is now the property of the Right Honorable George Talbot Rice, Baron Dinevor) situated on the top of a lofty eminence, surrounded by beautiful woods, and lands laid out with exquisite taste, which, with an elegant modern mansion house, form together a most pleasing assemblage of delightful objects, thence near Golden Grove, (the seat of John Vaughan Esq Lord Lieutenant and Custos Rotulorum of the county of Carmarthen) thence, by the Bishop's palace near Abergwilly, and the foot of Llangunnor Hill, on to the town of Carmarthen, thence near Rhydgorse, Pibor, (the seat of Rich le Davids, Esq) Towy Castle, (the property and residence of the Rev Mr William Evans) and afterwards by Llanstephan castle, until it empties itself into the sea, a few miles below the ancient borough of Kidwelly In this long course the Towy, originally small, receives into its channel various rivers and small streams, rendering it, in consequence of such accessions, navigable from Carmarthen quay to the sea, for vessels of 200 tons burden

And

And mount thee o'er thy common bounds,
'Till delug'd are the lowland grounds!
Of threat'ning danger soon aware,   25
The farmer acts with cautious care,
And from the valley drives away
His cattle, sheep, and corn, and hay,
Left in a sad, unguarded hour,
The waters should the whole devour.   30
Such well-tim'd prudence brings its gain,
And oft prevents a life of pain!

With pensive contemplation fir'd,
And love for gloomy shades inspir'd,
Thoughtful I bend my lonely way,   35
And to Llangunnor's church-yard stray,
Where rows of lofty ash are seen,
And solemn yew trees, ever green!
Where o'er the graves some stones appear,
Which tell whose bodies moulder there;   40
Whilst other marbles, long since plac'd!
Are by the hand of time defac'd.
Where double graves appear, and shew
Mothers and infants buried low,

Ver 36] In this church-yard is a stone over the grave of Dorothy, the wife of Griffith John, who died on the 30th of August 1759, at the advanced age of 102, a remarkable instance of longevity in modern times.

Ver 43] The double graves here spoken of, require explanation Upon the top of the mother's, the shape of a small grave, resembling

The firſt, in child-bed, borne away, 45
The laſt, too weak behind to ſtay
For young and old muſt, ſoon or late,
Abandon life's deluſive ſtate,
And rich, and poor, and low, and high,
Muſt here, together blended, lie! 50
Equality, like this, is juſt,
For all muſt crumble into duſt!

But think not that my peaceful muſe,
With pleaſure, doctrines ever views,
Such as in blood-ſtain'd France abound, 55
Which all diſtinctions would confound,
And to an equal level bring
The humble peaſant and the king,
Which would the rich man's wealth divide,
As rapine's horrid force ſhould guide 60
Tumultuous mobs, whoſe mighty will
Is there the rule of action ſtill.

---

an infant's, is formed by ſtones neatly placed there, and which are always kept white being occaſionally waſhed with lime water They ſhew a reſpectful attention paid to the memory of the deceaſed by their ſurviving relatives However, it is much to be lamented, that this attention is often fruſtrated by the unfeeling practice, too common in Wales, of turning horſes and hogs into the cemetery, to depaſture the graſs, when they unavoidably trample on the graves of the ſilent dead This cuſtom, in the emphatic language of our moſt celebrated bard, " would be more honored in the breach, than the obſervance "

Should

Forbid it heav'n! for in my mind
The man, whose thoughts are thus inclin'd,
Should ne'er in this fair island stay, 65
But march like graceless Paine away.
Unfit to live, (with truth I sing!)
Beneath so mild, so good a king,
As (ev'ry loyal tongue must own)
Now glorious fills the British throne, 70
Or seek protection from our laws,
Which well deserve our best applause
Oh! happy Britons! who ne'er know
The miseries from war that flow,
But, widely distant from its seat, 75
Secure an undisturb'd retreat
Within your native, blest domains,
Where sweet domestic comfort reigns!
Shall France indulge her ancient hate,
And undermine her rival-state, 80
And you, brave Britons! not unite
To do your injur'd country right?
Ah! rather in one mighty band
Arise, and join with heart and hand,
Like your forefathers, nobly brave! 85
Your best prerogatives to save,
And your old sanguinary foes,
With strongest efforts to oppose.

Ver 87] Alludes to the French, and the horrid decree passed some time since by the convention, not to give the English prisoners any quarter!!!

Thus,

Thus, by one common int'reft bound,
Your bafeft enemies confound,   90
And fhield, from fell deftruction's jaws
Your king, your liberties and laws.
Thus, danger fhall be diftant hurl'd,
And thus you may defy the world!

    The loyal ardor of the mufe,   95
This long digreffion muft excufe,
For tho' with patriot zeal fhe burns,
She, duteous, to her theme returns.

    Whilft near the church-yard wall you ftand,
The lovely landfcape to command,   100
What charming beauties ftrike your fight,
And yield a ravifhing delight!

    Behold the meadows, clad in green,
Where various lowing herds are feen,
Devouring, fome, the tender blade,   105
And fome, who full repafts have made,
Reclining on the verdant foil
To chew the cud, whilft others toil
In leading home, from ftubble fields,
The produce which each fruitful yields. 110
View fome employ'd in drawing lime,
The fallows to manure in time,

Ver 95] Altho' the digreffion requefted to be pardoned may
be deemed by critics too long, yet as it arifes out of the fubject,
the author hopes for indulgence on the grounds mentioned in the
text. See the conclufion of the note on verfe 416

Whilst there the goading driver, now,
Makes others trail the useful plough,
See those, whom teazing flies invade,   115
For shelter, occupy the shade,
And others, to avoid the heat,
Seek in the stream a cool retreat.

In the rich foliage of the year,
Cystanog woods! full cloath'd appear,   120
Where birds combine, with varying notes,
Proceeding from their tuneful throats,
To form far sweeter melody,
Than human song, or catch, or glee,
And teach vain mortals to be gay,   125
And pure and innocent as they.

Beneath those woods, see Towy's streams
Reflecting back Sol's noon-tide beams,
Enriching thus the pleasing view,
And to old beauties adding new,   130
And as you look, both far and near,
The river's windings still appear!
Of human life, an emblem true,
As any author ever drew,
For thence may thinking mortals know   135
The changing state of things below,

            And

Ver. 136] The man whose education has been liberal, can readily overcome those groveling considerations, and ordinary motives, by which the mistaken world are generally actuated

            When

And that each flatt'ring prospect here,
Which serves the heart of man to cheer,
May vary, like the turning stream, 140
Or prove, at best, an idle dream!
Set your affections, then, on high,
Where your immortal part must fly,
For there shall stable joys abound,
And everlasting bliss be found!

The valley and its prospects bright, 145
To observation next invite,
And there Cystanog-house descry!
The fertile lands which round it lie!
And Bishop's-Palace! (late the seat
Of Horsley! eminently great! 150

When he reflects, that even from the instant he first entered into this transitory state of existence, he was intended for immortality, tho' formed with a body liable to decay, he will accommodate his temporal views accordingly, and not make provision for eternity with perishable matters. When a man adopts this principle for the regulation of his demeanor here, the pursuits of ambition and avarice will become as insignificant and contemptible as the amusements of children, and the advantages of honors, pleasures, or of wealth, will not deserve to be considered as the primary objects of his enlightened mind.

Ver. 145.] This ancient mansion is situated in the parish of Llangunnor, and was formerly the property and residence of Thomas Vaughan, Esq.

Ver. 149.] This palace is situated near Abergwilly village, and is the usual residence of the bishop of St. Davids. The present bishop is brother of the Earl of Bute, and lately succeeded the now bishop of Rochester, on his translation to that see.

Endow'd

Endow'd with strong and nervous sense,
Ably applied in faith's defence,
And, in the mystical dispute,
Thy doctrines, Priestley, to confute.
Long shall each humble curate raise   155
His voice, with gratitude to praise
The feeling pastor! kind and good,
Who his best benefactor stood,
And, high among the sons of fame,
Shall, Horsley, place thy honor'd name.)   160

The tall surrounding trees between
Fam'd Castle-Piggin's seat is seen,
And Penybank hides not its head,
Though now its ancient charms are fled.
Save that its grove of beauteous oaks,   165
Has bow'd not to the woodman's strokes,

Ver 152] Alludes to the letters addressed by the present bishop of Rochester to Doctor Priestley, on the subject of the Holy Trinity, and the divinity of our blessed Saviour

Ver 155] Refers to the generous concern felt by the late bishop of St Davids for those curates in his then diocese, whose stipends were extremely small, and which he caused to be augmented

Ver 162.] This seat is in the parish of Abergwilly, and was formerly the property and residence of Mrs Gwynne, relict of Richard Gwynne Esq It is now in the possession of Thomas Blome, Esquire

Ver 163] This mansion-house is also in the same parish, and was lately sold by Lady Anne Hamilton.

But foon or late beneath his axe
Muft fall, and pay life's common tax!
The church and village intervene,
And fill up this perfpective fcene.   170

More diftant, eaftward, caft your eyes,
Where yonder craggy cliffs arife,
Upon whofe topmoft fummit bold,
There Druflwyn-Caftle you behold,
And in the intermediate fpace,   175
Unnumber'd beauties you may trace,
For turn whatever way you will,
Some lovely profpect opens ftill!

See hills o'er hills, alternate rife,
Whofe fummits feem to touch the fkies   180
And Pen'ralltfawr amongft the reft,
Uplift its cultivated creft,
Whilft in the charming valley nigh,
Delightful objects meet the eye.

Ver. 169] Reprefents the parifh church and village of Abergwilly, both near the bifhop's palace.

Ver. 174] This caftle is in the parifh of Llangathen, and is fituated upon an eminence which overhangs the river Towy. It belongs to Mr Vaughan, of Golden Grove. The caftle is now in ruins, a few of the old walls only remaining entire.

Ver 179] The Brecknockfhire hills, feveral others at a diftance, and fome which furround Llangunnor, are feen from thence.

Ver 181] This hill is in the parifh of Abergwilly.

There

There Allt-y-Gôg appears in sight, 185
Clad, like fair truth, in purest white,
And in each well selected spot,
Behold some peasant's peaceful cot,
To which, whene'er his labors close,
At eve, with pleasure sweet he goes 190
To sooth the partner of his care,
And with her ev'ry comfort share,
Whilst his dear offspring eager burn,
To welcome their lov'd sire's return,
And to partake the envied bliss, 195
Proceeding from his fervid kiss,
Or, deck'd in smiles, they anxious flee
To mount and dandle on his knee.

Such joys, ye swains, are yours alone,
How rarely to your betters known! 200
Rich in content, though small your store,
Your heav'nly Father you adore,
On him a firm reliance place,
A pattern for each higher race!
On him for all your wants depend, 205
The rich and poor man's equal friend!
Who kindly listens when we call,
And bounteous blessings pours on all!

The corn which lately wav'd its head,
Whilst growing in its native bed, 210

Ver 185] Allt-y-Gôg is also in the parish of Abergwilly, and belongs to George Morgan, Esquire, late high sheriff of Carmarthenshire

To man has been compell'd to bow,
Whose sickle since has laid it low;
And, by the labor of his hands,
Behold! in num'rous stacks it stands
Arrang'd in yonder spacious fields,   215
Where smiling plenty, transport yields.

 The humble gleaners too! descry,
Picking the scanty ears that lie
Dispers'd along the furrow'd land,
But gather'd with a careful hand.   220
Oh! husbandmen! when Ceres yields,
Rich, yellow harvests in your fields,
Some bowels of compassion shew,
For those poor objects, full of woe!
(Partakers of your nature still,   225
Let pride distinguish as it will!)
Who scarcely have the means to live,
To them a lib'ral handful give,
And Boaz-like the boon impart,
Urg'd by the dictates of the heart!   230
Such charity, I must maintain,
Is not bestow'd by you in vain,
For God, whom all the good adore,
Will, tenfold, multiply your store!
Thus up in heav'n a treasure lay   235
Against the awful judgment-day!

Ver 229] See the book of Ruth, chap ii ver 14 et seq.

Nearer the spot on which you stand,
Observe the patient angler's hand
Swing round his line, and skilful try
To catch, with artificial fly, 240
Those fish in Towy which abound,
And where may constantly be found
Salmon, with scales of silver hue,
And suin, glitt'ring like the dew,
The eel, quite difficult to hold, 245
And full as slippery as gold,
The darting trout, with crimson dy'd,
And various other sorts beside.

Behold, where yonder stubble lies,
To which the whurring partridge flies 250
At morn and eve, by dint of call,
Repeated by the covey all,
The wants of nature to supply,
Unconscious that there's danger nigh.
But mark the sportsmen with their net, 255
With silent steps the place beset,
Where these poor birds a short repast
Partake, now doom'd to be their last!
For, lo! the setters in the wind
The strongly perfum'd breezes find, 260
And dropping down, as early taught,
Shew where the covey may be caught,
O'er which th' entangling net's dispos'd,
And ev'ry single bird's inclos'd.

Below the hill see Gwilly stray, 265
Obedience to its chief to pay,
And into Towy's channel pour
Its waters ev'ry fleeting hour,
For homage to the great is due,
And Towy, to that maxim true, 270
Submits in turn, and onward flows,
To satisfy the debt it owes,
Surrend'ring its first stock and gain,
With mild obeisance to the main.

The church-yard quit, and to the brow 275
Of Park-yr-Eglwys hasten now,
And stopping where the quarry lies,
Beauties unsung arrest your eyes!

Beneath the spot where lately stood,
On the declivity, an wood, 280
See white-wash'd Dan-yr-Allt appear,
And Towy gently flowing near.

Ver. 265] Gwilly is a small river which rises in Carmarthenshire, and discharges itself into the Towy, near the foot of Llangunnor hill.

Ver. 275] Means Llangunnor church-yard, from whence, north of the church, the view already delineated may be taken.

Ver. 276] Park-yr Eglwys, signifies in English, the Church-field: it is also called Llanvawr.

Ver. 277] The quarry is immediately under that corner of Park yr Eglwys, which adjoins the declivity mentioned in ver. 280.

Ver. 281] Dan-yr-Allt, which in English signifies, under the wood, is in the parish of Llangunnor, and is the property of John Lloyd Esq. of Plymouth.

Beyond it, through the fir-tree grove,
Where taste and skill have nobly strove
To add to nature, beauties still, 285
See, from the leat of yonder mill,
The frothy water, wild and strong,
With rage impetuous dash along,
And o'er its stone-pav'd channel glide,
(Resistless as the flowing tide) 290
Forming as lovely a cascade
As human efforts ever made.

Above, and not far distant, view
That Villa, beautiful and new,

Ver 283] The grove adjoins the leat conducting the water employed in turning various wheels, belonging to works, mentioned in a subsequent note From this leat all the waste water empties itself along a channel formed thro' a shelving bank The bottom of the channel is paved with large stones, placed in such order as not only to afford a very powerful resistance to the stream, but also to improve the effect of its fall The late proprietor of the works, (whose taste contributed to ornament his landed property in and about Carmarthen) very judiciously left a breach in the wall adjoining the turnpike road at the entrance into the town, opposite the cascade, which breach is filled up with an iron railing, and thro' this the fall of the water is seen, and has a striking effect but not so gratifying as the more distant view it exhibits to a spectator stationed on Llangunnor hill

Ver 294] This modern and elegant Villa was lately erected by John Morgan Esquire, of Carmarthen, the present proprietor of the works, for the residence of his principal agent, Mr Philip Vaughan

With

With shrubberies about it plac'd, 295
And trees dispos'd with nicest taste.

Behind it, on the upland ground,
There Penlan mansion-house is found,
If with a nice discerning eye,
The half-hid object you'd descry. 300
How green the fir-trees standing near,
In various groups and clumps appear!

Now let the eye (descending deep,
Near where the river takes a sweep)
Survey the furnaces, which stand 305
With other works, by artists plann'd,
There constant industry prevails,
Sure source of wealth, which never fails!

Behold the beautiful parade,
By art and nature jointly made, 310

Ver 298] This house belongs to Mr. Morgan.

Ver 305] The furnaces and other works here alluded to, belong to Mr Morgan, and are used for smelting and running iron ore into bars, and for manufacturing tin plates. Near these works John Campbell, Esq of Stack-Pool, in Pembrokeshire, (member for Cardigan borough) lately built a furnace for smelting lead ore, raised from his estate near Llandovery

Ver 309] The parade is a walk made by subscription under the direction of John Williams Esq of Wenallt, (late high sheriff of Carmarthenshire) when mayor of Carmarthen

Where

Where lovely women charm the eye,
And unsuccefsful lovers sigh.
Well has a pleasing poet said,
Who long from this vain world has fled,
" No females can with ours compare, 315
" So chaste, so innocent and fair.
" The trav'llers oft, who transient view
" Their matchless forms, have cause to rue
" The magic of their piercing eyes,
" From which love's pointed arrow flies, 320
" And, fix'd directly in the heart,
" Occasions all a lover's smart.
" Thus strangers are compell'd to own
" They sigh for nymphs to them unknown."

From Park-yr-Eglwys' brow descend, 325
And down the slope your footsteps bend,
Till Erw Frân you slowly gain,
Where hillocks deck the shelving plain.

Thence Llwyn-y-Gwragedd Hill appears,
Where oft his hounds the huntsman cheers, 330
When early in the blushing morn,
He sweetly winds his bugle horn,

Ver 313] The poet here alluded to, was Mr Phillips, author of a poem called Cyder, written in blank verse

Ver 327] Erw Frân, in English, Crow's Acre, is the next field but one below Park-yr-Eglwys

Ver 329] Llwyn-y-Gwragedd Hill is in the parish of Llangunnor.

And casts his dogs round yonder brakes,
To which the hare for shelter makes,
Whene'er stern winter's shiv'ring storm   335
Requires a refuge snug and warm
Yet what avails this close retreat?
For then the hounds approach her seat,
Directed by the well-known trail,
And with loud notes her ears assail.   340
(Music to sportsmen ever dear,
Who love such harmony to hear,
But to the fearful, panting hare,
Productive only of despair!)
Yet though by foes encompass'd round,   345
She cautious quits the dang'rous ground,
And flies o'er distant hills and fields,
Till, wholly spent, her life she yields
With piteous squeakings, which impart
No pleasure to the tender heart: 350
But sportsmen's hearts resemble steel,
And rarely soft compassion feel
For the four-footed timid race,
The harmless objects of the chace:
Thus the poor hare unpitied dies,   355
And useless are her piercing cries!

 Near the preceding hill descry
The works which at its bottom lie,   Where

Ver 358] The works here spoken of are lead mines. Messrs. Marsden's and company, of Carmarthen, and another company, are now driving different levels, intended to drain off the water, and
to

Where bold advent'rers, under ground,
Expect great riches may be found, 360
And certainties well-pleas'd resign,
To search for veins of deep-laid mine,
Upheld by hope's inviting smile,
Too apt our prospects to beguile!
But small successes have their use, 365
And to good fortune oft conduce

Still to the view fresh objects rise,
To gratify the wand'ring eyes,
And, lo! Maeslan, (beside the wood)
Where, erst, an humble cottage stood, 370
Presents its front, and, in the rear,
See, o'er the grove, Tyllwyd appear.

Now to the south inclining more,
Unnotic'd prospects you explore,
But, first, White-House, where, long since, dwelt 375
A bard, whose bosom often felt,

to approach the main body of the ore; the quality of which is extremely fine, well adapted for the use of potters, but contains little silver

Ver 369] Maeslan, in the parish of Llangunnor, is the property of Mr William Bonville, of Carmarthen

Ver 372] White-House, in that parish, was formerly the residence of Sir Richard Steel, having belonged to his lady. It was afterwards purchased by Mr Lloyd, of Plymouth, from Sir Richard's daughter, the late Lady Trevor.

And made the breasts of others feel
Poetic fires, Sir Richard Steel!
And there the ancient orchard view,
Where he his "Conscious Lovers" drew.   380
Hard fate! that he, (who virtue taught,
And vice to check, incessant sought,
Who, as a Christian Hero bold,
Man's ev'ry duty did unfold,
And, by his own example, prov'd   385
In life he by his precepts mov'd,
Whose writings ne'er shall know decay,
Till time itself shall fade away,)
Should silent moulder into dust,
Without a monument or bust,   390

Ver 379] Tradition (in general a faithful recorder of facts) says, that Sir Richard Steel actually wrote, or completed, his comedy of the Conscious Lovers in an arbor, in the orchard adjoining White-House, and to enable him so to do, and to superintend the management of the Llangunnor and other estates to which (upon the death of his lady in December 1718) his daughter became entitled, it is extremely probable that he came to White-House on his return from Scotland, where he went as a commissioner of the forfeited estates in September 1720. He did not arrive in London after that journey, 'till March 1721, or thereabouts, and this is confirmed by a note in the first volume of his Epistolary Correspondence, page 139, by which it appears, the Conscious Lovers remained unfinished 'till 1721. The editor of that work has not been able precisely to ascertain where or when this comedy was completed, which greatly supports the traditional account. Sir Richard actually resided at White-House, and removed from thence to Carmarthen where he died, and was buried in that Church.

Ver 383] Sir Richard wrote a tract called the "Christian Hero."

Ver 390] No monument was ever erected to the memory of Sir Richard in Carmarthen church.

To guide the living's curious eye,
And point out where his ashes lie!

Sweetly attractive! mark the spot,
Where, further distant, stands a cot,
For simple neatness justly fam'd,   395
And with due taste, Mount-Pleasant nam'd.

Next, in the west, (near yonder trees,
Which wav'd are gently by the breeze)
Behold, between the earth and sky,
Carmarthen church-tow'r, mounted high.   404
Hark! hear you not that solemn bell?
Some rich or poor man's parting knell!
If heard aright, its sound must bear
Important tidings to your ear,
And to your heart a warning give,   405
That here you can't for ever live,
But must expect to yield your breath,
When summon'd by resistless death
Oh! awful change! may we with care,
For the last solemn hour prepare,   410
When life our earthly frames shall leave,
And to our God our souls would cleave,
Mounting aloft, with active wing,
To heaven, to praise its mighty King.

Ver 396] Mount-Pleasant, in the Parish of Llangunnor, is the property of the Rev. Mr Evan Holliday, of Carmarthen.

> To earth returning (her laft flight 415
> My mufe affum'd in Johnfon's fpite)
> There with delightful pleafure view
> Carmarthen town, both Old and New,
> The place where Merlin claim'd his birth,
> That mighty prophet when on earth, 420
> Who

Ver. 416.] Doctor Johnfon, in his Criticifm on Denham's Cooper's Hill, feems to condemn the too frequent introduction of moral or ferious reflections in that poem; but with due deference to an authority fo great, it is fubmitted that when fuch reflections, whether moral or otherwife, arife naturally out of the fubject-matter of the work, they are not unaptly introduced, but ferve to remind us of the inftability of all human enjoyments, and that we ought not fo to live here, as to forget that we are to live hereafter. Mr. Warton (author of an Effay on the genius and writings of Pope) in his examination of Windfor Foreft, obferves, that " it " is one of the greateft and moft pleafing arts of defcriptive " poetry, to introduce moral fentences and inftructions in an " oblique and indirect manner, in places where one naturally " expects only painting and amufement, and that it is this par-" ticular art which is the diftinguifhing excellence of Cooper's-" Hill, throughout which, the defcription of places, and images, " raifed by the poet, are ftill tending to fome hint, or leading " into fome reflection upon moral life or political inftitution." A line of Mr. Pope's, of the interrogative kind, may, perhaps, not inapplicably be added here, fubftituting one word only inftead of another.

" Who fhall decide when CRITICS difagree?"

Ver. 418.] Old and New Carmarthen were incorporated together by a charter, granted by his prefent majefty, in the 4th year of his reign.

Ver. 419 et feq.] The birth of Merlin, at Carmarthen, and the reputation of his having been a prophet, are fpoken of by
different

Who in Allt-Fyrddin form'd a cave,
Which serv'd him for his house and grave
His wants were truly few indeed,
But few are those which mortals need!

Lo! where yon castle boldly stands,   425
And tow'rs above the neighb'ring lands,
Around its turrets and old walls,
See how the twining ivy crawls,

different ancient authors Vide Camden's Britt by Dr Gibson, vol 2 p 774 et seq There is a prophecy concerning Carmarthen, said to be uttered by Merlin (who was also called Myrddin, and from whom the town is supposed to have taken its name) in the Welsh tongue This prophecy is repeated from memory by many of the Welsh inhabitants of the place, and being curious and short, it merits insertion here.

Original
" Caerfyrddin, cei oer foreu,
" Daear a'th lwngc, daw dw'r yn dy le "

Translation
" Some dreadful morn, Carmarthen shall deface,
" O'erwhelm'd in earth, floods shall supply its place "

Ver 421] Allt-Fyrddin, in English Merlin's-Wood, is situated on the side of a lofty hill, in the parish of Abergwilly Merlin's cave, in that hill, is, to this day, shewn to the curious

Ver 425] Alludes to Carmarthen castle, which has long been the county gaol It was twice visited (last, in May, 1788) by that humane and amiable man, the late Mr Howard, in consequence of whose reports, the gentlemen of the county (actuated by feelings congenial with his own) did, by authority of parliament, raise money to defray the expence of making such additions and improvements as had been suggested by Mr Howard, which were begun in 1789, and finished in 1792, under the direction of Mr. Nash, an eminent architect, in Carmarthen

Supporting by its friendly aid,
What mould'ring time has much decay'd: 430
His scythe permits not aught to stand,
Design'd to feel his iron hand!

Below the town direct your eye,
And there Carmarthen bridge descry,
Which serves to join each sever'd shore, 435
And waft the passing trav'ller o'er
The river, which those shores divides.
A barge now through the main arch glides!

Behold those ships! moor'd near the quay,
Whose streamers in the north-wind play, 440
And with the influx of the tide,
See vessels on its bosom ride,
And likewise those prepar'd to go
To sea, when back the waters flow
Thus did the great Creator's pow'r, 445
(Whose glory should be sung each hour!)
When first this lower world he plann'd,
The work of his almighty hand,
Ordain, that twice in ev'ry day,
The tide should his commands obey, 450
That men of commerce ne'er might fail
To waft abroad the swelling sail.

Ver 434] This bridge is of stone, very ancient and strong, and consists of seven arches. It has a pleasing appearance when viewed from Park-yr-Eglwys.

Ver 439] Alludes to Carmarthen quay

Upon the glitt'ring stream behold
Those fishermen, of courage bold,
In num'rous pairs, pursue their trade   455
In coracles, themselves have made,
Form'd of slight twigs, with flannel cas'd,
O'er which three coats of tar are plac'd:
Those vessels, when made water-tight,
They use for fishing day and night,   460
And with a paddle, to and fro,
Against or with the stream they go,
Leading a net, held by one hand,
Whilst t'other does each bark command.
Thus ample draughts of fish they take,   465
And thus an honest livelihood make,
And (as a porter bears his pack)
Each mounts his vessel on his back,
When first his usual work's begun,
And when his fishing toil is done.   470

See, in the west Job's-Well appears!
Whose recent owner, young in years,

Ver. 468] It may appear extraordinary to those who have never seen any coracles, that fishermen should carry them on their backs, but surprise will cease, when it is asserted as a fact, that the largest of these vehicles does not, in weight, exceed forty pounds, or thereabouts.

Ver. 471] Job's-Well is in the borough of Carmarthen. Its late proprietor, Thomas Jones, Esq. died at the early age of eighteen. He was a young gentleman of very promising abilities, and intended, had he lived, to have been called to the bar.

By cruel death's unerring dart,
Was doom'd with life and friends to part,
Ere tears had wholly ceas'd to flow 475
For his lov'd father, levell'd low.
Great, matchless man! my muse would raise
A lasting tribute to his praise,
Had she, proportion'd to her will,
An ample share of genuine skill, 480
His worth and virtues to rehearse,
In grateful, though in humble, verse.
He, strong and polish'd sense possess'd,
A heart, with mild compassion blest,
Pure attic wit, which, as it flew, 485
The loudest peals of laughter drew,
A lib'ral and expanded mind,
To social happiness inclin'd,
For in his hospitable dome,
Ev'n strangers felt themselves at home! 490
Of honor pure, of judgment clear,
A tender parent, friend sincere,
For strict integrity admir'd,
And with the love of justice fir'd,
Deeply acquainted with our laws, 495
In which he practis'd with applause,
And (to compleat so fair a plan)
He liv'd and died an honest man.

Ver 476] Alludes to the late Thomas Jones, of Carmarthen, Esq the preceding owner of Job's-Well. He was universally beloved whilst living, and, dead, will long exist in the recollection of his surviving friends.

The chosen subject to pursue,
Behold Treberfed full in view 500
Below the summit of the hill,
And nearer, by Pontcarreg mill,
See yonder lovely cottage plac'd,
Whose wings display improving taste!

A thousand other pleasing views 505
Might claim attention from my muse,
But these she wishes to resign,
To celebrate a spot divine,
For one remains which baffles more
Description, than those mark'd before, 510
Which now, in all its splendor bright,
Each ravish'd eye fills with delight!
See, near the river's charming banks,
Those fir-trees, planted out in ranks,
Where yon high double-mansion stands, 515
Surrounded by delightful lands,
And Allt-y-Knap a back-ground forms,
To shield it from tempestuous storms.
Oh, sweet Rhydgorse! enchanting seat!
Oft times a skilful bard's retreat, 520

Ver 500] Treberfed is also in the borough of Carmarthen. It was formerly the property of the Rev. Mr. David Scurlock, late of Blaencorse, in Carmarthenshire, and now belongs to Mr. James Hughes.

Ver 503] Alludes to a neat cottage, lately erected by David John Edwardes, Esq. of Carmarthen.

Ver 571] Allt-y-Knap is a hill in the above borough.

Ver 519] Rhydgorse is the property of Mr. David John Edwardes,

When (from contemplating the law,
Which keeps the good and bad in awe,
From courts, where righteous men preside,
Who follow justice as their guide)
He, in each long recess retires, 525
To write whate'er his muse inspires.
Thus various studies are combin'd,
And occupy his active mind.

Here ends my task! for, lo! the sun
His daily course has nearly run, 530
And my exhausted muse would fain
Retire, fresh vigour to obtain,
Content, that she first bent her will,
In verse to paint her favourite hill,
And its best prospects to explore, 535
Which please, when oft'nest seen, the more.
On these sweet scenes might genius gaze,
And mark the landscape with amaze,
'Till, lost in rapturous delight,
His pow'rs descriptive take their flight, 540
And from his hand, enfeebled then,
Down drops the pencil, or the pen.

Edwardes, and has been in the family for many centuries back, as appears by ancient documents in his possession. It was built on the scite of an old castle, called by the same name noticed in Powell, Wynne, and Warrington's Histories of Wales.

Ver 520] Alludes to a student in one of the inns of court, the author of a poetical epistle, addressed to James Boswell, Esq in 4to and published in 1790.

FINIS

Ingram Content Group UK Ltd.
Milton Keynes UK
UKHW051200300323
419408UK00009B/645